Reading Success Mini-Books

SIGHT WORDS

Twenty Interactive Mini-Books That Help Every
Child Get a Great Start in Reading

by Mary Beth Spann

SCHOLASTIC
PROFESSIONAL BOOKS

New York ● Toronto ● London ● Auckland ● Sydney ● Mexico City ● New Delhi ● Hong Kong

Cover design by Jaime Lucero

Interior design by Ellen Matlach Hassell
for Boultinghouse & Boultinghouse, Inc.

Illustrations by Maxie Chambliss

ISBN: 0-439-10440-8

Contents

Introduction

Welcome to *Reading Success Mini-Books: Sight Words*. This book provides a fun and easy way for young children to experience early sight words. Beginning readers will really benefit from completing and collecting all 20 of these little books. When used as a regular part of a balanced approach to literacy—one that includes reading, writing, speaking, and listening—the books will provide children with an easy-to-understand, concrete foundation for print mastery and vocabulary development.

Research tells us that children learn letters and words best when they're presented in a meaningful context. Each sight words mini-book introduces children to a group of simple, illustrated words that feature the same thematic thread. Each one offers children the chance to practice writing and reading these words, and provides a simple review activity so children can test themselves on what they've learned.

The books' small size means they are a breeze for young students to complete, store, collect, and keep. They help give children a sense of mastery and ownership over the words they are learning. In a way, these mini-books serve as the children's own print-awareness progress reports. As children successfully work through the books, it's easy for them to see how each one represents an important step on the road to reading.

Assembling the Mini-Books

1. Make a double-sided copy of the mini-book pages.

2. Cut the page in half along the solid line.

3. Place pages 4/5 on top of pages 2/7 as shown.

4. Fold the pages in half along the dotted line.

5. Check to be sure that the pages are in the proper order and then staple them together along the book's spine.

How to Use This Book

This book contains 20 six-page mini-books, one for each of 20 popular early-elementary themes. How you introduce and share these books with children will largely depend on how you introduce thematic studies and sight words in general. But no matter how you use them, you'll find these books to be small but powerful page-turners. Here are some ideas for putting them to work in your classroom:

Pre-assemble Mini-Books as Needed

Instead of asking children to assemble these books in class, you may want to assemble a complete class set ahead of time. This prep-step allows students to focus their attention on the mini-books' content, rather than on construction. Remember: Parents who are unable to volunteer in the classroom may welcome this task as something they can work on at home.

Let the Books Serve You

Here are some quick tips for making the mini-books a successful part of your reading routine:

- If you introduce thematic activities to the whole class, you might introduce the mini-books in that same manner. Each student, or small groups of students, may then work on the same theme mini-book simultaneously.

- For a more individualized approach, in which each child approaches sight words at his or her own rate, you may make the books available to children on an "as needed" basis. Perhaps you can set up a thematic display stocked with a supply of corresponding mini-books. When individualizing, keep a mini-book checklist showing which ones each child has completed. Be certain to schedule student/teacher conferences so you can assess and celebrate children's progress.

- As children learn how to read and spell the words in the books, consider transferring the words to thematic word wall lists. Invite children to write and illustrate additional words for each list. Encourage children to refer to their mini-books and/or word walls when writing stories and books of their own.

Recommended Read

In his comprehensive resource book, *Phonics From A to Z: A Practical Guide* (Scholastic Professional Books, 1998), reading expert Wiley Blevins recommends a phonics sequence for introducing letters and sounds. Because this must-have book offers explanations and rationales for all aspects of phonics instruction, it is very helpful in guiding the use of phonics mini-books.

Introducing the Mini-Books in Class

1. Show children how a book is constructed and what they are expected to do on each page.

2. Work through one mini-book together.

   a. Read the cover together. Demonstrate how to use the "Name" line. Call attention to the configuration of the letters printed there.

   b. Call attention to the picture and word on each page. When children correctly identify a picture by reading the word, invite them to explain their reading strategies. In doing so, you are asking children to pay attention to the print features of the word below the picture.

   c. Demonstrate how to copy the word on the line provided. Suggest to children that if they think they already know how to spell the word, they can try and cover the word below the picture and write the word without peeking.

   d. Show how the back-cover activity serves as a self-checking review page. (Tip: The back cover can also serve as a screening page. If you suspect a child already knows how to read, spell, and write all the words in a mini-book, you can ask him or her to complete this page before completing the whole book. That way you'll know if the child needs to move on to a mini-book that is at a more appropriate instructional level.)

Mini-Book Extensions

- Meet periodically with each student to review mini-books together. To organize their mini-book collections, give each child a large metal loose-leaf ring. Punch a hole in the upper left-hand corner of each completed mini-book and slip each one onto the ring. Store collections in a multi-pocketed shoe bag (hanging on the wall or from a door-knob), or hung on wall hooks.

- A tree trunk and branches decorated with a few paper leaves makes a nice bulletin board backdrop for displaying new books (before adding them to the rings). Just tack individual books to the branches so they resemble leaves. Title your display "Leaf Through a Mini-Book!"

- Set aside class time for children to take turns sharing one book of their choice.

- Designate one day a week as "Mini-Book Take-Home Day" so children can share their growing library with family members.

- Provide blank mini-books so children can write and illustrate their own thematic-word collections, perhaps related to a favorite hobby, sport, or area of interest.

Generating Family Support

1. When familiarizing families with instructional materials and strategies you plan on using to teach reading and writing, introduce phonics mini-books as part of your overall approach.

2. Emphasize that a well-balanced program includes phonics plus many other strategies for reading, speaking, listening, and writing with children. Share specific examples of how you include these components in your program.

3. Invite families to extend learning at home by reading aloud together everyday, by calling attention to any written material that fills their days, and by reviewing school work—including mini-books—with their children.

Write a new back-to-school word. Then draw a picture to go with it.

_____

- - - - - - - - - - - - - - - - -

_____

8

My Book of Back-to-School Words

_____

- - - - - - - - - - - - - - - - -

Name _____

I

book

_____

- - - - - - - - - - - - - - - - -

6

school bus

_____

- - - - - - - - - - - - - - - - -

3

backpack

_____

- - - - - - - - - -

_____

2

pencil

_____

- - - - - - - - - -

_____

7

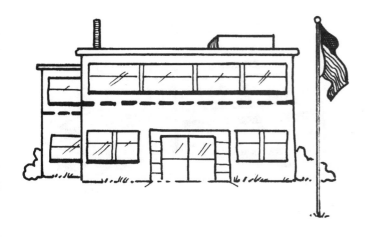

school

_____

- - - - - - - - - -

_____

4

teacher

_____

- - - - - - - - - -

_____

5

Write a new fall word.
Then draw a picture to go
with it.

_____
- -
_____

8

Reading Success Mini-Books: Sight Words   Scholastic Professional Books

My Book of
Fall Words

_____
- -
Name _____

1

scarecrow

_____
- -
_____

6

pumpkin

_____
- -
_____

3

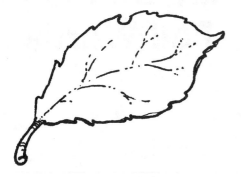

leaf

- - - - - - - - - - - -

2

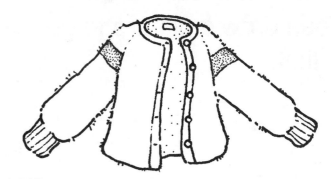

sweater

- - - - - - - - - - - -

7

apple

- - - - - - - - - - - -

4

rake

- - - - - - - - - - - -

5

Write a new weather word.
Then draw a picture to go
with it.

_____
- - - - - - - - - - - - -
_____

8

Reading Success Mini-Books: Sight Words   Scholastic Professional Books

My Book of
Weather Words

_____
- - - - - - - - - - - - -
Name _____

I

cloudy

_____
- - - - - - - - - - - - -
_____

6

rainy

_____
- - - - - - - - - - - - -
_____

3

sunny

2

foggy

7

windy

4

snowy

5

Write a new birthday word.
Then draw a picture to go
with it.

_____

- - - - - - - - - - - - - -

_____

8

Reading Success Mini-Books: Sight Words   Scholastic Professional Books

My Book of Birthday Words

_____

- - - - - - - - - - - - - -

Name _____

I

present

_____

- - - - - - - - - - - - - -

_____

6

candles

_____

- - - - - - - - - - - - - -

_____

3

cake

2

friends

7

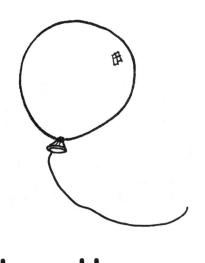

balloon

4

hat

5

Write a new Halloween word.
Then draw a picture to go
with it.

_____

- - - - - - - - - - - - - - - - - -

_____

8

Reading Success Mini-Books: Sight Words   Scholastic Professional Books

My Book of
Halloween Words

_____

- - - - - - - - - - - - - - - - - -

Name _____

1

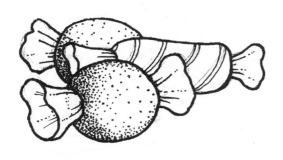

candy

_____

- - - - - - - - - - - - - - - - - -

_____

6

witch

_____

- - - - - - - - - - - - - - - - - -

_____

3

ghost

2

bag

7

jack-o'-lantern

4

costume

5

Write a new farm word.
Then draw a picture to go
with it.

_____

- -

_____

8

Reading Success Mini-Books: Sight Words   Scholastic Professional Books

My Book of Farm Words

_____

- -

Name _____

1

sheep

_____

- -

_____

6

cow

_____

- -

_____

3

barn

2

pig

4

horse

7

chicken

5

Write a new Thanksgiving word. Then draw a picture to go with it.

_____

- - - - - - - - - - - - - - - -

_____

8

My Book of Thanksgiving Words

_____

- - - - - - - - - - - - - - - -

Name _____

Reading Success Mini-Books: Sight Words   Scholastic Professional Books

I

stuffing

_____

- - - - - - - - - - - - - - - -

_____

6

Mayflower

_____

- - - - - - - - - - - - - - - -

_____

3

Pilgrims

_____
- - - - - - - - - - - - -
_____

2

Native Americans

_____
- - - - - - - - - - - - -
_____

4

corn

_____
- - - - - - - - - - - - -
_____

7

turkey

_____
- - - - - - - - - - - - -
_____

5

Write a new winter word.
Then draw a picture to go
with it.

- - - - - - - - - - - - - - - - -

8

My Book of
Winter Words

Reading Success Mini-Books: Sight Words   Scholastic Professional Books

----
- - - - - - - - - - - - - - - - -
Name _____

I

snowman

- - - - - - - - - - - - - - - - -

6

boots

- - - - - - - - - - - - - - - - -

3

mittens

2

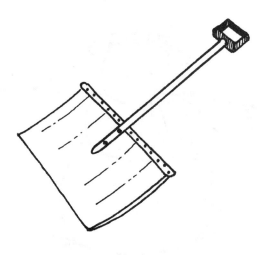

fireplace

7

snow

4

shovel

5

Write a new penguin word.
Then draw a picture to go
with it.

_____
- - - - - - - - - - - - - - - -
_____

8

My Book of Penguin Words

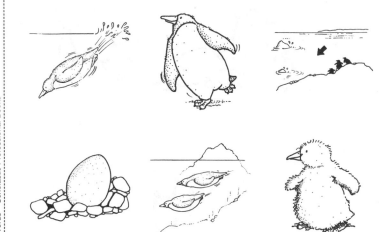

_____
- - - - - - - - - - - - - - - -

Name _____

Reading Success Mini-Books: Sight Words   Scholastic Professional Books

1

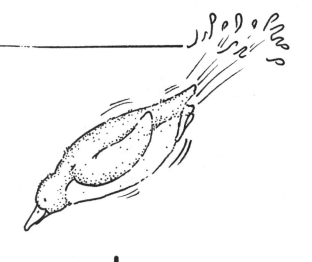

_____

dive

_____
- - - - - - - - - - - - - - - -
_____

6

chick

_____
- - - - - - - - - - - - - - - -
_____

3

egg

_____

- - - - - - - - - - - - - - -

_____

2

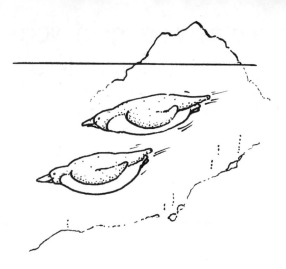

swim

_____

- - - - - - - - - - - - - - -

_____

7

waddle

_____

- - - - - - - - - - - - - - -

_____

4

water

_____

- - - - - - - - - - - - - - -

_____

5

Write a new Valentine's Day word. Then draw a picture to go with it.

_____

_____

8

My Book of Valentine's Day Words

Name _____

Reading Success Mini-Books: Sight Words Scholastic Professional Books

I

flowers

_____

6

cupid

_____

3

Valentine

_____

- - - - - - - - - - - - - - -

_____

2

love

_____

- - - - - - - - - - - - - - -

_____

7

card

_____

- - - - - - - - - - - - - - -

_____

4

chocolates

_____

- - - - - - - - - - - - - - -

_____

5

Write a new community
helper word. Then draw a
picture to go with it.

_____

_____

8

Reading Success Mini-Books: Sight Words   Scholastic Professional Books

My Book of Community Helper Words

Name _____

_____

1

doctor

_____

_____

6

police officer

_____

_____

3

teacher

_____

‒ ‒ ‒ ‒ ‒ ‒ ‒ ‒ ‒ ‒

_____

2

librarian

_____

‒ ‒ ‒ ‒ ‒ ‒ ‒ ‒ ‒ ‒

_____

4

mail carrier

_____

‒ ‒ ‒ ‒ ‒ ‒ ‒ ‒ ‒ ‒

_____

7

fire fighter

_____

‒ ‒ ‒ ‒ ‒ ‒ ‒ ‒ ‒ ‒

_____

5

Write a new fruit or vegetable word. Then draw a picture to go with it.

_____

- - - - - - - - - - - - - - - - - - - -

_____

8

My Book of Fruit and Vegetable Words

Name _____

1

Reading Success Mini-Books: Sight Words   Scholastic Professional Books

celery

_____

- - - - - - - - - - - - - - - - - - - -

6

banana

_____

- - - - - - - - - - - - - - - - - - - -

3

apple

2

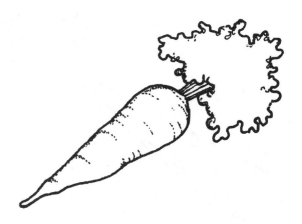

tomato

7

raisin

4

carrot

5

Write a new transportation word. Then draw a picture to go with it.

_____
- - - - - - - - - - - - - -
_____

8

Reading Success Mini-Books: Sight Words   Scholastic Professional Books

My Book of Transportation Words

Name _____

I

airplane

_____
- - - - - - - - - - - - - -

6

bus

_____
- - - - - - - - - - - - - -

3

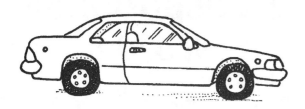

car

2

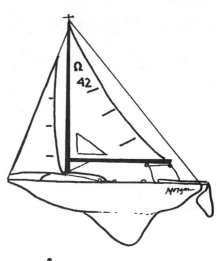

boat

7

taxicab

4

train

5

Write a new clothing word.
Then draw a picture to go
with it.

8

My Book of
Clothing Words

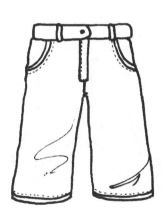

Name _____

I

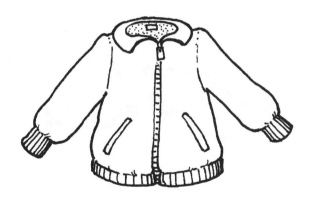

jacket

6

pants

3

Reading Success Mini-Books: Sight Words   Scholastic Professional Books

shirt

_____

2

hat

_____

7

socks

_____

4

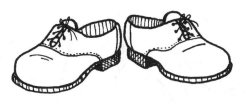

shoes

_____

5

Write a new pet word.
Then draw a picture to go
with it.

_____
_____

8

My Book of Pet Words

Reading Success Mini-Books: Sight Words   Scholastic Professional Books

_____
Name _____

1

hamster

_____
_____

6

dog

_____
_____

3

cat

_____

- - - - - - - - - - - -

_____

2

fish

_____

- - - - - - - - - - - -

_____

4

snake

_____

- - - - - - - - - - - -

_____

7

rabbit

_____

- - - - - - - - - - - -

_____

5

Write a new forest animal word. Then draw a picture to go with it.

_____

_ _ _ _ _ _ _ _ _ _ _ _ _ _ _

_____

8

My Book of Forest Animal Words

_____

_ _ _ _ _ _ _ _ _ _ _ _ _ _ _

Name _____

1

Reading Success Mini-Books: Sight Words   Scholastic Professional Books

owl

_____

_____

6

raccoon

_____

_____

3

squirrel

_____

- - - - - - - - - - - -

_____

2

bear

_____

- - - - - - - - - - - -

_____

7

deer

_____

- - - - - - - - - - - -

_____

4

rabbit

_____

- - - - - - - - - - - -

_____

5

Write a new spring word.
Then draw a picture to go
with it.

_____

_____

8

My Book of Spring Words

_____

Name _____

1

rain

_____

_____

6

nest

_____

_____

3

eggs

_____

- - - - - - - - - - -

_____

2

umbrella

_____

- - - - - - - - - - -

_____

7

chick

_____

- - - - - - - - - - -

_____

4

flowers

_____

- - - - - - - - - - -

_____

5

Write a new bug word.
Then draw a picture to go
with it.

_____

- - - - - - - - - - - - - - - - - - - -

_____

8

Reading Success Mini-Books: Sight Words   Scholastic Professional Books

My Book of Bug Words

_____

- - - - - - - - - - - - - - - - - - - -

Name _____

1

spider

_____

- - - - - - - - - - - - - - - - - - - -

_____

6

ant

_____

- - - - - - - - - - - - - - - - - - - -

_____

3

ladybug

_____

2

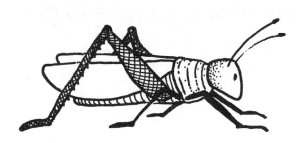

grasshopper

_____

7

bee

_____

4

butterfly

_____

5

Write a new plant word.
Then draw a picture to go
with it.

_____
- - - - - - - - - - - - - - - - -
_____

8

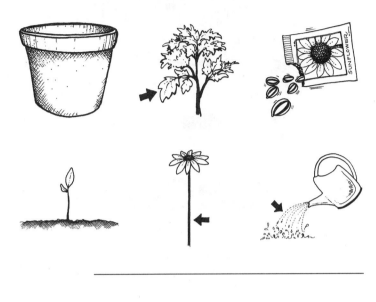

stem

_____
- - - - - - - - - - - - - - - - -
_____

6

pot

_____
- - - - - - - - - - - - - - - - -
_____

3

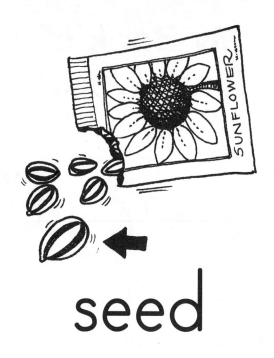

seed

2

leaf

7

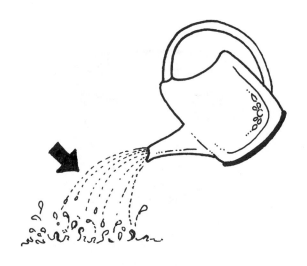

water

4

sprout

5

Write a new summer word.
Then draw a picture to go
with it.

‗‗‗‗‗‗‗‗‗‗‗‗‗‗‗‗‗‗‗‗‗
- - - - - - - - - - - - - - - - - - -
‗‗‗‗‗‗‗‗‗‗‗‗‗‗‗‗‗‗‗‗‗

8

Reading Success Mini-Books: Sight Words   Scholastic Professional Books

My Book of Summer Words

‗‗‗‗‗‗‗‗‗‗‗‗‗‗‗‗‗‗‗‗‗
- - - - - - - - - - - - - - - - - - -
Name ‗‗‗‗‗‗‗‗‗‗‗‗‗‗‗‗

1

pail

‗‗‗‗‗‗‗‗‗‗‗‗‗‗‗‗‗‗‗‗‗
- - - - - - - - - - - - - - - - - - -
‗‗‗‗‗‗‗‗‗‗‗‗‗‗‗‗‗‗‗‗‗

6

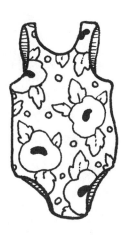

bathing suit

‗‗‗‗‗‗‗‗‗‗‗‗‗‗‗‗‗‗‗‗‗
- - - - - - - - - - - - - - - - - - -
‗‗‗‗‗‗‗‗‗‗‗‗‗‗‗‗‗‗‗‗‗

3

sun

ice cream

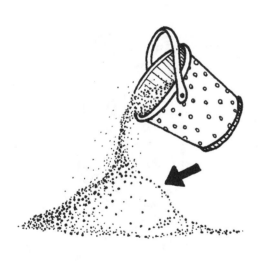

sand

umbrella